EARTH SKY

I0200802

studiokav.com
amsterdam

Published by studiokav
7 7 2 1 9 4 0
Ferdinand Huyckstraat 38
1061 HW Amsterdam
The Netherlands
info@studiokav.com

ISBN: 978-90-814933-4-5

Typeset: Book Antiqua
CoverArt: Leslie Kavanaugh © 2014
Book Design: AAK

CONTENTS

Leslie Jaye Kavanaugh

EARTH SKY

EARTH SKY

Earth Sky

Seemingly motionless

The limitless border between the sky and the earth

Is but an obscure moment

The universe, too, has it's time of entreaty,

Beseeching the void to endure.

Yet with a clamor and a deafening grief,

The Still and the Quiet

Will come to an apotheosis

Of shining absence

Mutely withheld

Weeping.

TIME IS MEANT

Time is meant to be spent,
Eaten up rapaciously, hungrily
For when it is over,
There will be no remains
Only the portion allotted to
Accomplish the fullness, without residue
Radiant and rare
So, even though we stand timorous
At the end station –
Drink the full cup, ample and complete,
intoxicated with life
  Until the very foam disappears,
  Until the wounded return
  Until the fulgurated rapture
In the fullness of time's tenderness.

THE LIGHTNING

The lightning rends a tear in the dark cloud
Reminiscent of the apocalypse
My father struggles to let go of life
Recalcitrant to the end, fighting
The deal: All that lives must die
No!
He is stubborn to the very threshold,
The rip
The knife's edge between what is known and
What is the Return.
From childhood to maturity,
He was always rebellious
Repeatedly thrown from the horse, but
Obstinately climbing back on
Determined to beat the odds,
To defy the deal;
A force of nature, my father, who
Refuses to die:

> Hold onto the mane of the wild horse
> Hold on whilst she rattles your bones
> Hold on even though you cannot breathe

You will live forever in my heart, indefatigable

> And, like my father, I stand up again,
> I survive the life without rectification;
> I slap the dust from his old blue jeans, and
> I ride.

TOGETHER

Together we plan to retaliate
Against the transitory nature of time
So we cling together,
Our bodies melded by desire,
Grasping, clasping, pressing
Life
Before it escapes in an instant
Before it is exacted by a moment.
And yet this urgency eventually
Succumbs to the inevitable:
To the evidence of the evening song
To the excruciating excess
Of nothingness passing.

THE CLOUDS

The clouds are in combustion
A fire that cannot be quenched
But pass by in orange and yellow
A chalice of gold
Holding the setting sun
Until we come full circle
Another day
Another closure
The sky embraced in a fervent pink afterglow
Ardent and feverish
Unceasing and fulgent
Flush and effervescent
Time occurring all blue and mellow
Not an end,
But a transition
Until we come full circle
Another night
Another completion.

THANKFULLY I HAVE FORGOTTEN

Thankfully, I have forgotten you

All those years ago.

I have forgotten the way you walk into a room as if
you own it;

I have forgotten your explosive laugh

albeit infrequent;

I have forgotten the smell of your hair in the morn-
ing;

I have forgotten the half-closed eyes late at night;

I have forgotten summertime on your skin;

I have forgotten the recognition in your countenance;

I have forgotten the small scar on your shoulder;

I have forgotten the bitten fingernails – but only on
your left hand;

I have forgotten your wild hair that refused to be
combed;

I have forgotten your rope-like muscular legs;

I have forgotten the sight of you earnestly reading
while I tried my best to disturb you;

I have forgotten the scratch of the old-fashioned pen
as you wrote me a poem;

I have forgotten your scowl at my impatience;

I have forgotten your stubbornness;

I have forgotten the fervent protests;

I have forgotten the persistence of your desire;

I have forgotten the solemnity of your responsibility;

I have forgotten your distant father in a far off land;

I have forgotten your all-too-present mother;

I have forgotten

I have forgotten

I have forgotten

I have forgotten your hands,

your hands in mine,

your hands on mine,

your hands;

I have forgotten your hands that never wore

a wedding ring;

I have forgotten the vastness of separation;

I have forgotten the futility of longing;

I have forgotten.

Thankfully, thankfully, I have forgotten you.

THE HILLS OF SHANE

The hills of Shane
In green time –
The ever-present wind
Captures my wheaten hair
Just as it blows
The long grasses
Leeward about my ankles and shins.
The hills of Shane
In green time –
Knew kings and slaves
Knights and their ladies
But I stand here forlorn,
Wondering when all will be forgiven
Vehemently hoping for peace
On the hills of Shane
In green time.

LEAVING

Leaving the lavender in Provence
Is a rift, a tear, a laceration.
Leaving the levies in New Orleans
Is a submersion, a grief, a lie.
Leaving the library in Alexandria
Is a betrayal, an abjuration, a lodestone.
Leaving the lock in London
Is a rebellion, a spike, a limit.
Leaving the lotus blossoms in Nara
Is a rending, a narrow, a litany.
Leaving the luminescence in Island
Is a call, a lightning, a lucidity.
Leaving the luxuriance in Bali
Is an orchid, a seduction, a liberation.
Leaving the lyricism of Ireland
Is a beat, a tie, a loneliness.
But leaving your love
Is a lifetime.

AWASH

Awash with liberty

Restless and free

Bearing signs of lasciviousness

And swollen with rounded fecundity

The young man smiled wistfully

Knowing in the manner of the invincibility of youth

Confident and wayward

Strident and edgy

Ah! That bluesy feeling of high summer

Where everything is in the fullness of possibility

Fragrant and easy

Swing unfettered and be free!

VIVID

Vivid and burning,
Weigh heavily on me
Lean on me
With your profundity
With your somber casting.
The sweet eternities of remembrance
The unmistakable languor of our ruminations
The winter came softly
And, never white, bearing thickly,
In the wake of pale,
The dawn is abundant
With immaculate trembling.

CENOTE

Diving into the cenote, blue
Crystal, magic world
Ancient world, cool embrace.
Swimming in the cenote with you
  How many life-times?
  How far?
  How deep have we gone?
Floating in your soul with you
Sparkling effervescent azure
Coming up for air occasionally,
But always touching bottom.
Your voice is kind of reminder
A plumbing of the depths,
A sonic vibration,
A harmonics as primordial as the world itself
Therefore I know that this sound
Was meant to sing with my voice
Mine had up until that moment,
A clear crystal tone
But I lacked the counter-point,
The warmth of the baritone
Yours, a cenote blue.

EACH AFTERNOON

Each afternoon, after a difficult rousing,

Hung over and sick

The poet would walk down to the small shed by the shore

And there he would try to drink coffee,

And if successful, a little whiskey,

And then maybe, slowly, amidst

      The disgust

      The despair

      The ever-present disquietude,

The poems would come.

HALF-WAY

Half-way around the world,
I travell ed
To see the cherry blossoms bloom
In Hangzhou
But I was too early;
The bamboo was growing,
The first suggestions of blue wisteria,
But the lotus still lay dormant,
Vendors selling fried soft-shell crabs on a stick
Alongside the Westlake;
Couples and families gathering on the
Moon Bridge,
Boat rides past the stone lanterns
Of the ancestors.
But I was too early;
Only the leaves on the cherry trees
Had started to greet the spring
So that the sight of the delicate pink blossoms -
Prized not only for their beauty -
But for their ephemerality,
Were missed in time
Transition, breathtaking, absent

All things pass

Even those things missed.

Stupendous

All things flow

Even time

When I returned home,

They had planted cherry trees in the garden

Outside of my window.

EVER INCREASING

In the ever increasing scope of my prison
Is there no place untouched by pain?
Repression and exile
Are but two sides of the same coin.
My internment is as wide as the steppes
And as deep as the duration.
Only Shostakovich's Fifteenth String Quartet -
What he called his "requiem" - can understand this
Alienation.
And there is no place untouched by malediction;
Wide-open and yet suffocated,
Airless in the desolate room,
These are but two sides of the same coin.
No man is completely free
Except possibly in his mind; and
Victory over tyranny is a battle rarely won.

HIS HAIR WAS BLACK

His hair was as black and tumultuous as
The river Shannon
And so was his truculent soul.
(Even his mother called him a "blackguard",
Although with a sparkling laugh
And a teasing lament).
Of course, I loved him with an inevitability that was
      Like falling down
      Like gravity with weightlessness
      Like a sweet trembling surrender
To say he broke my heart would be an
Understatement -
He just took my life
      Down, down in the depths
Of the turbulent river Shannon
And there I drowned in his relentlessness
Within the tumult alongside the mill factory;
Until I could no longer distinguish
The tormented rush of the dark waters from
      The white pale of my flesh.
The black, black of the river Shannon.

I AM JUST

I am just trying to figure it all out...
The semi-permeable obscurity
Like an ivory-white immovable flux
Surrounds me like a vaporous fracture
Finite and final
Confusion resounds
Questions remain unanswered,
Indeed, are perhaps unanswerable
Impenetrable as the fecund fog
Tinctures of wind
Blowing fiercely without purpose or direction
Into the fragile future
Into the tenuous filament.

I AM THE WIND

"I am the wind," she thought.
The wind blowing through my hair is no different than
The wind coursing down the canyon.
The sun on my back is the same as
The sun warming the rock on which I am sitting.
The wind and the sun are the one
Constant in the ever-changing desert.

HE GAVE

He gave me a blank book
I did not know whether to write in it
Or draw in it.
But I was pleased
The emptiness seemed to be

      An invitation to fulfillment

      A possibility

      A promise.

And I dreamed of love poems written to him
And I imagined paintings of my life shared with him
Yet none would transpire in the end
The white page prevailed.

SCINTILLATING

Scintillating rainfall
Punctuates fiercely the interior calm.
Gathered around the evening fire,
Toasting chestnuts, warm and fragrant
The sonorous play of water upon the roof
Only adds rhythm to your sighs.
As I recline by your side,
Grandmother's quilt 'log-cabin'
Keeps us in safe repose
Amidst the storm savage.

I HAVE WALKED

I have walked down this road too far to go back now

Every choice brings me into a new

Clearing – a new wide open

Space that is not necessarily clear

Clarity only comes later with

Reflection

Ever-remittent

Paths that are not necessarily obvious

When walking, when merely putting

One foot

In front of the other

Because, however quixotic, I never know

Where I am truly going

So I remain for a while

No regrets

We return to the pavilion to drink tea.

FIELDS OF FLAX

Fields of flax,

Ochre and sepia

Frame the fragments of

Time's remembrance

When the harvesting comes,

The reapers float upon

The sea of fruition,

Seemingly like foam upon the gold

Life goes on:

Perpetuating and persevering -

The ever-recurring and

Fluent language of Life.

I LOOK DOWN

I look down at the skin on my arm
And suddenly I see
My mother's skin -
Freckled and crêpe-like,
Silken folds revealing cerulean blue veins.
She is driving the car in summertime
And I am beside her
Jumping out of my adolescent skin,
Tanned and velvet-like,
Taut cover, impatient and smooth.
I did not look upon her with generosity then
Wondering how long before she would become like
Her mother's skin.
Pleated and linen-like,
Draperies elegantly gathered upon her
Diminishing frame.
I look down at the skin on my arm
And suddenly I see
My mother's skin.

FIGHTING AGAIN

Fighting again for a place -
A nest out from which I can fly
I have built this house
Stick by stick
Mud brick by stone
Marking out my location in the world
The place from which I can exist
Home is man's essence
Hearth is man's eternity
I pull the purple wool shawl
Closer around by shoulders.

FORGED

Forged with recollection

Burnt with memory

Your letters are stacked in a positive architectural pile

Each on blue air post stationary

Sent from afar

Sent to a destination not longer attainable

My heart.

Where is that man who wrote poetically

     Of forever

     Of love eternal

     Of passion aflame?

Each letter grown transparent and

Fragile with age,

Searching to arrive at tender redemption,

To arrive at sweet forgiveness.

HE STARES

He stares at the whisky in front of him
Is the liquid poison? Or sweet respite?
Gold and amber light reflects upon
His tawdry companion
But they attend only to the drink.
This tavern is for the 'professional' drunks –

    No pretense of amusement,

    Only the daily wretched share

The color is long faded
The tedium is long entrenched
Only waiting for the page to turn,
Waiting for the perfect balance

    Between the all-too-sober reality

    And the gut-wrenching disgust

Only waiting,
Only waiting for the burnished and rectified.

STAND FAST

Stand fast
Stand firm against the vicissitudes.
The only certainty is that everything changes
The only finitude of life is that
All will cease to be.
Everything that is born must die
But this does not mean that I
Embrace this wretched truth;
The inevitable is ripped from my finger tips
My hands grope ever-insistently
For the moment of understanding
Until I succumb to the nocturnal membrane.
I will withstand the unalterable,
Approaching silence
With tenderness, with puissance, with resplendence
But never submission.
Everything that is born must die, yet
Nothing that dies will escape the delirious rapture.

THESE

The song that is growing dim
The night that is enlarging into time
The friends who have marched into the abyss
The day that is already dawn
The graveyard that is newly sown
The memory that is clothed in ochre shadows
The knowing that remains unfulfilled
The leaving that is never undone
These, these, you bequeath to me.

INDEED

Indeed, encapsulate my finality
In your sweet sanguinity.
In your midst, I have lived
In succulent plenitude.
And yet vaguely voracious,
The resplendent end, irreversible and ever-insistent,
Coming before my eyes luminous
Burnished in gold
In fragrant obscurity;
The interminable approaches
To devour me in fierce tenderness.

INDIAN INDIGO

Indian indigo skies shrouding shoulders

In the expanse

In the place where the tribes gathered

So long ago.

Now only the wind coalesces

Coming and going

Just as easily as the divinations themselves.

Every man thinks he will live forever

But the ruins on the ridge

Attest otherwise

Yet the sun still shines on the plains

The graves of my forefathers.

AWAKENED

Awakened by a cover of mist
My mind is slow to comprehend
The rising morning from the deepest blue-black night
From whence did I come?
And whence will I end?
And upon this narrow threshold
My thoughts did suspend
Between the eternal and the present behold
What is this place "I am"? and
What universe will transcend?

ALL THE WAY DOWN

All the way down here
All the way down to the bottom
Here is my confusion
Here is my negation
Here is my transformation.

IN THE RAVAGES OF TIME

In the ravages of time, Thanatos,
The god of death
Waits patiently
Exacting every kind of suffering
Unwavering in tenacity
Never fluctuating
Never forgiving

In the redemption of time, Eros,
The god of the life-giving
Interrupts the destruction
Feverishly forestalling
Ever fervently
Ever fleshing
Erupting in fragile fulfillment.

JUST SIT

"Just sit", he commanded;
"Just plow your own patch", he admonished.
Only this can an artist do.

"We are only dropping a few breadcrumbs
On the path so that we can
Find our way back", he proffered.
Only this can a philosopher do.

"But then the bastards come and eat them!",
I protested.
"Not bastards: that is just the way of the world",
He corrected.
Only this can a poet do.

PUT ON A SILENCE

Put on a silence
      Like a cloak
      Like a cape
      Like a sadness
Put on this silence
That no one can speak
Darken over the corners
Straighten the transgressed edges of memory
In the midst of the indecipherable
Withstand the accursed soundlessness
Put on a silence.

THE SAGE

The sage knows that the truth is ineffable.
Even if he could bring words to the unalterable
Speech would fail him.
The inexhaustible infinitude
Presses upon his soul.
The wise know that loving wisdom
Is not the same as
Possessing wisdom,
Intangible and often inaccessible.
Therefore the seeker is always
Inoculated against truth's infringement
Immaculate.

MAN STANDS

Man stands with his back to the wall
And calls himself 'free'.
But the mighty forces rush at him incessantly,
Insistently
Try as he might, he is unable
To repel evil
And fortunately he is also equally unable to shun
The light of compassion
As they say, 'the sun shines equally upon
The evil and the good'.
But when he comes to the wisdom
That all his attempts at virtue have come to nothing
He shall despair
For he knows the gods are
Not to be manipulated,
Even by good deeds.
Whence will his prayers go?
To which destination will his pleas be directed
When the only thing a man can do
Is stand?
Stand with a certain pride
A certain resolve
A certain free-will
Just stand.

SUCCULENT

Succulent curvature of your shadow
Is not to be delayed
Vivid unwinding of celestial domain
Is not to be avoided.

A LOVE STORY WITH THE UNIVERSE

You know there are some who would call me a life-hog
I scream out, falling to my knees
Dying to take it all in.
To let the universe own me is my condemnation;
Men among men,
Love among man
Journeying together, joined
To the delectable desire
And then he loved me.
He calls me to the light;
I who has only known the darkness,
The cool dampness of ignorance is like a cave
That holds me in womb-like comfort.
But the comfort is an illusion
I bleed out and scream out of my being
I long for the light;
That which I do not imagine -
Dare to desire the unknown
and surrender to love forgiving.

TURGID

Turgid waters
Torrential storms.
Our safe harbor is suddenly threatened.
Nature will prevail while
Man seeks his permanence
In the transitive
In the destructive
In the slender need of hope
Turning around again
Trapped in the inevitability of fate.

IN EXTREMADURA

In Extremadura, the drunken gods whisper maliciously,
In this land where Nothingness prevails
The burden is stony but invisible

    Like gravity –

    Always present

    Oppressive

Swollen with conception,
Forged with a hammer
In the center of the earth
Brimming crucible:

    Bury the burden

    Burn with rage

    Burnish the resentment

Until polished bright,
It alights unto the sky
And with the scorched shards of the earth:

    Descend down into the canyons

    Detour down into the crevasse

    Dig down into the caverns

Until bathed in sweat,
The gods fall silent
Until my forehead burns
On the border, in the far, to nowhere.

WALKING

Walking underneath Willink's pergola

Cold night permeates the atmosphere

Perfumed blue

Treacherous presentiment

In the distance, mawkish beasts

Gather ominously

Planning an act of perfidy

Onerously hanging about

Persistent and pervasive

The azure sky persists as a portent,

The fetid clouds providing no protection

For the approaching and oncoming evil to appear -

Oppressive and pernicious.

TIME'S SILENT BURDEN

Time's silent burden

Is knowledge.

Time's eternity

Is wisdom.

Just as inevitable

Is the memory that

Forgets only to remember.

The time of yesterday

When love was as broad as the horizon

And as frenzied as quintessence.

Gracious floating out of time's limit

Time's duration

Is a lamentation.

YOUR INCOMMODIOUS HEART

Your incommodious heart has known
Innumerable betrayals –
The walls brook no infringement
Even desire does not make it porous
Forever insular –
When will you allow someone to love you?
I stand against the insurmountable -
My arms wide open
Chest bare pressing upon your chest
My legs firmly standing against your legs.
I am going nowhere
Until the insidious fears are dissolved
For we are inseparable
Just in need of reparation, and
Just like South Africa, in need of reconciliation.
Please, please heart,
Accommodate me.

LAY ME DOWN

Lay me down on a bed of green moss
In the small wood.
The lower meadow, surrounding, is high
      With cornflowers,
      With Queen Anne's lace,
      With clover.
The sun is roused upon your rising face;
The spottled light is dancing upon your eyes.
And in our little sanctuary amidst the ferns,
      I want to live forever
      In your arms
      In your heart.
As the fragrant respite of warmth envelops us,
As the full fecundity of summer enfolds us,
As the fierce intensity of desire encompasses us.
Softly, green, down in the small wood.

A LONE WOMAN

A lone woman walked along the abandoned fields
Winter weighed upon her mourning
Her head wrapped up in white wool
Appearing just above the distant horizon line;

The last light of day lay upon her shoulders
And she stopped a moment,
Hesitating in the approaching gray,
Whilst the sky lit up in a parade of light

A fervent array, magnificent
On the way to visit her husband's grave
To grieve; to pray, and
Not far away, stones sticking up like the feet of

Corpses black against the copula gray,
A glimpse into the lapse of time,
A somber display,
Futile tears on the edge of the sky.

MOUNT FUJI

Mount Fuji always conceals her secrets
The moment is shrouded in mists
But Mount Olympus overwhelms
The domain of the gods
Shows man his righteous place
If only he opens his eyes
The mythos is revealed.

DOES NOT NEED

God does not need my servitude,

My obedience

God does not need my love

For god is love, and

Any love I might direct towards a god

Is indeed

Not separate from that which is love,

God

LIFE

DIAPHONOUS DIFFUSION – I

With a mere breath
We come into this world
Still but a gossamer being
Becoming fine, floating on the
Good graces of life itself
Until such a sparse moment
That we breath and
Escape the subliminal labyrinth of non-being
And at once defy the grip of death
Swimming up into consciousness
Like from a cenote translucent emerald
Still but a precarious being
Becoming soul permeated, spreading out and
Dispersing from the tissue of the Undifferentiated
Diaphanous diffusion.

CACOPHONOUS CADENCE – I

Stepping full into the chiaroscuro

Enclosure of living

I forget my origins

I forget my vulnerability

I attempt to forget that this life is but a chimera

A coarse crucible for purifying the soul

And listen instead to the clamorous chatter

The cloud of mere noise that descends upon my mind

Often craven and crude,

Pulls me off my crystal course

My immaculate completion

My full circle.

And in this cavern of chaos

I forget the capacious certitude

Of the divine amidst the

Cacophonous cadence.

LUMINOUS LEAP –I

With lamentations I regret,
Having escaped the labyrinth
I have fallen into the calamity of the chimera
      The blinking multi-chromatic clamor
      The chasm of chaos
      The vast confusion
Distracted and distanced
Devising a daedal plan to land upright
      To fly above the seeming disorder
      To become wise
      To stand with pride
Like a true human being who is also divine.
The inner spirit shines the light on the way,
But only one step at a time
For man never knows what lies ahead
Only the 'here' and 'now':
The future is only fear and projection
Yet I create it with every poem
Struggling through the cragged crevasse
I come to the edge of the abyss
Luminous leap.

MIRACULOUS MANIFEST – I

Awakened and aroused
In the luminous dawn of enlightenment
Surging ahead and yet going nowhere
Wearing a magenta mantle
For a few mere moments
I am unbidden and unbound
Arising into a vault resplendent
Lustrous and narrow
The margins of my 'self' merge with that of
The magnificent vessel
The multitudinous multiplication of the same
Manifold modulations coming on in waves
Was Spinoza correct?
Separation is a mistake
Was Parmenides correct?
Being is One
Was Plotinus correct?
One is All.
Miraculous manifest.

DIAPHONOUS DIFFUSION – II

When deliberately descending into life
The Soul cannot be accused of ignorance
The sea is murky
The sky is all a mist
The horizon is unclear
Milky but middling
So that the delineation between
Heaven and earth is a vague vault
The entry a mere fissure
Into the world unknown
A tidal wave of endurance
Enervating with the stream
Ruled by the seasonal moon
The mind settles into time
Into a lifetime
Diaphanous diffusion.

CACOPHONOUS CADENCE – II

Now fettered and grasping
Like all the other souls in this delusory world
I listen to the heartbeat
I listen to the herald
I listen to the honorable.
A mere child in this resounding discord
Soon disoriented
The course is in a tumult
The chorus is in an uproar
The chime is inharmonious
Loud voices calling upon an uprooted soul
Unanswered, the outcry begins
The early hours gather;
The virgin hearse glides by
The dissonant din grows.
Cacophonous cadence.

LUMINOUS LEAP –II

Time is unsegmented
Chronology is a continuum
No beginning; no end
And mankind is but a border
A transgression in the totality
Yet despite this temporal face,
Life often goes unheeded
From moment to moment
Adding up to Nothing
Until the time of the unfolding
Portent and potent
Pregnant and productive
The push into the vast inexhaustible
Boundless un-falling
Sparkling immensity
Luminous leap.

MIRACULOUS MANIFEST –II

Only diffusion is possible

Not division

All is One

This unity has been the wisdom of sages for recorded time

My 'life' but a mere marker;

My 'self' but a mere margin;

My 'will' but a mere motive.

The truth is that I am married to the many

To All the world

Undifferentiated

Returning as an eternal mandate

To the magnanimous whole

Variegated, diverse, but not separable;

      I am the magnitude

      I am the merciful

      I am the mantle.

Miraculous manifest.

DIAPHONOUS DIFFUSION –III

From Nothing

I return to Nothing

Death is but an edge in time

Coming in

Going out.

What is to fear

When we have nowhere to go?

In the continuum of time

All is One

Life becoming a-live

And returning to Life

From one Form

I return to the Form-less

Breathe in

Breathe out

Diaphanous diffusion.

CACOPHONOUS CADENCE –III

In the early hours
I try not to harken
To the vociferent:
The outcry of the crowd
Merely masks the silences of the soul
The cry of injustice
The appeal to the non-existent gods
The rage against the lawlessness
In the emerging pale
I attend to the lugubrious lullaby
To the murmur of truth
Which can only be heard in solemnity:
The whisper ever melodious
The vertex of lucidity
The forest of chanting trees.
Listen!
Cacophonous cadence.

LUMINOUS LEAP –III

My weariness is immeasurable
I cling to life but I do not know why
I am holding onto illusion
I am grasping an empty concept
I am struggling against a wall of pain
Why?
This is the question every human
Must ask
Must answer
Why?
I still defend the false separation
I still tenaciously hold onto the "I"
I still firmly act as if I believe in matter
Despite the evidence to the contrary
Why?
To possess the truth down to the
Last
Luminous leap.

MIRACULOUS MANIFEST – III

Rapturous and radiant rare

When the final vestiges of un-truth

Are burnt from the souls

Burnished smooth and gold

All will be as it has always been

One

And always will be

One

Timorous and transparent tenderness

When the breath becomes as pure as a diamond

Sparkling clear and proud

The destiny will be revealed to be

Nothing

And the penultimate place to be

Nowhere

Miraculous manifest.

EARTH SKY 2

Every step connects me to the earth

Every breath is part of the sky

Green ferns silently expand their frothy wings.

And in unfolding

Return to earth/sky.